BEAUTY
for
ASHES

BEAUTY
for
ASHES

Transformed Through God's Love

TORRA HARRIS

TATE PUBLISHING
AND ENTERPRISES, LLC

Published by Tate Publishing & Enterprises, LLC
127 E. Trade Center Terrace | Mustang, Oklahoma 73064 USA
1.888.361.9473 | www.tatepublishing.com

Tate Publishing is committed to excellence in the publishing industry. The company reflects the philosophy established by the founders, based on Psalm 68:11,
"The Lord gave the word and great was the company of those who published it."

Published in the United States of America

ISBN: 978-1-62746-875-6
1. Religion / Christian Life / Women's Issues
2. Religion / Christian Life / Personal Growth
13.07.03

Acknowledgments

I give all praise and glory to God above for entrusting me with the experience and gracing me with the honor to share my story.

I am grateful for my spiritual parents Supt Clarence & Evangelist Cynthia Brown for laying a solid foundation and mirroring the image of a Christian. Thanks to the Mothers of Greater St. Paul COGIC for their encouragement and prayers. To Prophet Daryl Brown thank you for allowing God to use you as His mouthpiece. And to the rest of my Greater St. Paul family, I love you all.

To my "home away from home" church family, Pastor Daryl & Lady Mitzi Flintroy and the City of Joy COGIC family, thanks for the warm welcome and show of love.

To the dynamic duo Elders Angie McNair & Carroll Watson and the women of Sisters Empowering Sisters (SES, Inc.), thanks for the "connection".

To my friends (too many to name) I love you all and appreciate you for your role you have played in my life. May God continue to richly bless you all.

To the Johnson family, words cannot express my gratitude and love for each one of you. I am a blessed woman to be a part of such a loving and supportive family.

Special thanks to my sisters Barbara Likely & Vickie Johnson you two have been my "backbone". I truly appreciate every sacrifice you each have made to show your support. Thanks for being a sounding board and source of encouragement. As I often say "everybody should have a sister like y'all". I love you ladies to "life".

Last, but certainly not least, to my sons DeVonte & Keinte Harris. I thank God for strengthening me and causing to be a "mother after His own heart". I am grateful for the bond we share and for the support you both give me. I love you guys much.

Foreword

"I'm gonna write a book", that's what Torra exclaimed to me one evening about two years ago. The words from my mouth were: "Go for it girl". Inside I chuckled and wondered how she would write a book when it seemed so obvious (I thought) that she just did not enjoy writing. She always solicited assistance when doing writing assignments. And, her contribution to her assignments was primarily editing.

My hidden skepticism based on my knowledge of Torra's penchant for shying away from writing totally vanished when I was offered a sneak peek into the contents of Beauty for Ashes. Torra masterfully recounts major events in her life in vividly compelling details. She communicates her emotional and rational thoughts as she bears some painful memories while coming to the realization that she was an abused woman in a volatile marriage.

Who knew? Behind her smile and spirited disposition was a mountain of devastation, shame and pain that caused her to question her appeal. She reveals feelings of worthlessness and often wondered "why doesn't he love me". Who knew that the life of the party was so tattered and torn? I didn't.

The first chapter of the book is appropriately titled "What's love got to do with it". The answer to that question is ultimately realized and answered. The greatest love of all is the love of God. Torra came to the knowledge of the truth. She has found peace and joy in Christ.

Her story serves as an example of how God's love conquers all. The love of Christ exudes from the pages of her book. When my sister realized that her worth was not entangled with man, she was able to embrace God's love and accept His gift of "Beauty for Ashes".

Barbara Likely

Contents

What's Love Got to Do with It?

"What's love got to do with it" was once a very popular song by Tina Turner. Love is a very strong emotion. It has caused some people to commit murder, some to steal, and others to lose their minds. Being loved by someone is a very good feeling. To have someone to nurture you and tell you how much you mean to him or her is desired by us all. Having another to esteem your feelings higher than their own is a treasure to behold. I now know of such a love. For the bible declares in St. John 3:16 "For God so loved the world that He gave His only begotten son, that whosoever believeth in Him should not perish, but have everlasting life". Jesus is love, for I can truly say that if it had not been for the love of God, where would I be? So to answer the question; I'll say love has everything to do with it.

I remember when I was in high school; we would have Bible study once a week. Mr. Desmond was the minister who taught the class. He would tell us about hell and how if we were not "saved" we would go there and burn forever. I was fearful of the place he described. I even shed a few tears at the thought of going there. But I was in "love" with a man. See back then the only sin I knew about was fornication and I did not want to give up my boyfriend. I recall saying, when I get married I am going to get saved.

That was (and still is) a common myth many of us have, we seem to think that time is in our hand. I continued to attend Bible study each week, heard about hell, cried about the thought of going there, yet continued to walk in disobedience.

After I finished high school the man I was in "love" with was deported back to his native homeland. I soon embarked on another relationship. Actually I meet this guy while my "love" was being detained here in the states, before he was sent back home. The relationship with this new guy developed very fast. We were married within months of meeting (for all the wrong reasons). I did not love him like that, and I am sure he did not love me. But my position at the time was that he looked good, I was falling for him, and I didn't want to invest 2 more years with someone else only for him to be deported (just crazy right). I remember the day we got married we went to the courthouse, had our nuptials, afterwards I went to work and he went home (how romantic). As a matter of fact my friend Shawn picked me up from work that night and I stayed to her mother's house. I was 19 years old and did not realize what I was getting into.

I became pregnant with our first son Devonte shortly after getting married. I assumed this made us a family (actually it did by definition) so I had to make it work. We eventually grew on each other (or so I thought). After having our son, it quickly became evident that his true identity was that of a player and a batterer. See I thought his jealousy and occasional fights meant, "he loved me" (boy was I wrong). "Wow" this is the first time that I admitted to myself that I was a victim of abuse. I never saw myself as a victim because it wasn't an everyday occurrence, he just mostly pushed, and I didn't have any bruises (oh yea except that one time, I will tell you about that later). Love can make you blind.

The First Time

I am sitting here trying to recall the first time he ever hit or pushed me and I literally draw a blank. Not because I have repressed it, but truthfully because I do not think it was that significant to me. Don't get me wrong I am not down playing domestic violence. But I am saying that while I can't recall the first time he struck me, I do however remember when he first cheated (at least when I first found out). In other words his breaking my heart held a better place in my memory than him hurting me physically (go figure).

I remember returning home after hanging out at my friend Muke's house for the day. He was so nice and quickly gave me the okay (which was out of character for him) to go out that night with my friends. I was so happy to have his "permission" I did not wonder why he was not auguring about me going. He left to go hang out with his brother and cousin (so I thought) and my "girls" Muke and Gennean came by and we went out. Hours later he picked me up from the club and we returned home. He was standing in the dining area talking to me and suddenly my eyes glimpsed something on his neck.

Stunned, I quickly moved in for a closer inspection. My quick pace had now turned into a full charge as I realized that it was a "hickey" or "passion mark". He seemed shocked, as if he was unaware that it was there. He bolted out the door and down the street. I got into the car and drove down the streets looking for him. I saw his cousin's girlfriend standing outside the club and asked "Have you seen Johnny?" "No, didn't y'all pass by here in the car together a little while ago" she responded. I was too embarrassed to tell her what happened. "Yea" I replied while driving off and continuing to look for him. My efforts to find him that night failed. I finally went back home. He did not return home that night. Looking back that was a good thing due to the state of mind I was in (God was shielding me even back then).

The next day I went to his brother's house looking for him. His brother's girlfriend came to the door and said he was not there. She invited me inside. I began to cry as I told her what had happened. She expressed her sympathy for me and proceeded to tell me how she had been "wronged" in relationships, so she knows how I feel. She then let me in on a secret; she knew who the girl was. I had to first assure her that I would not let anyone know that she told me. She proceeded to tell me who the girl was. She again expressed her sympathy and how he was making a big mistake because he has a "nice family". I would later find out that the girl was her best friend and that house was their regular meeting place.

I was shocked, hurt, angry, and felt betrayed. This man who claimed he loved me. How could he do me this way? Did he not know that love was not supposed to hurt you? Little did I know that was just the beginning of the pain that I would experience for loving him.

Here We Go Again,
and Again

As hurtful as the first incident was, I stayed. I am sure he apologized and assured me that it would not happen again. So, we made up and I tried to forget about it. Several months after recovering from the humiliation of the first incident I was "blindsided" again.

This time I was at home and decided to go to his brother house to see what he was up to (woman's intuition). His brother and cousin lived in the same apartment complex a couple of doors from one another. When I came up the stairs I went to the cousin's door first (truthfully he could have been doing his dirt at either place). His nephew who was staying at the cousin's house told me that he was not there. He then proceeded ahead of me to the brother's apartment. In retrospect he was probably trying to warn him. Anyway, we get to the door; he knocks and slowly turns the doorknob. I went into the apartment behind him and there they were. He was sitting on the couch (with his hands, protectively folded across his lap) and she was sitting on the floor in front of him. Both were looking like a deer caught in headlights. I foolishly asked,

"What are you doing to Johnny". "Nothing" she replied. And yes, you guessed, a fight ensued. I do not know why I was so eager to fight her. I mean after all she never made a commitment to me. But at that time I figured, I'll get her now because I can get him later. Again I allowed him to apologize and promise that he would change. He had made a mistake (again).

The next episode happened several months later. One night while I was out partying with my friends I saw our car parked at his brother's place. I moved the car from in front of the building and put it in the parking lot across the street. I then went into the club and convinced his brother that I needed to go to his house to use the restroom. While he reluctantly came along, he became confident after seeing the car was no longer in front of the building. He put the key in and started opening the door, I pushed past him and went to the bedroom door and kicked it open. They were sitting on the bed and both jump up harmoniously. I grabbed the girl and the fight was on.

Did I mention that this all began after the first year of our marriage and lasted into the second year (with this particular girl)? I do not know why I stayed with him. But over the course of the year I had either caught them or heard about them being together. The "straw that broke the camel's back" was when she and he got into a big fight. This was the worst of the worst. Someone called me and told me what was happening. I went up to his brother's apartment building to see what was going on. When the girl saw me she became even more infuriated and tried to break loose from her friends. She started cussing me, calling me stupid and some other choice names, which I no longer care to mention. She then said, "Did he tell you that I was pregnant and lost the baby". I was devastated; I could not say a word. One of the officers on the scene asked me if I could leave since I appeared to be the "leveled headed one". Little did the officer know that it was my pleasure to leave after being embarrassed in such a manner.

This time publicly humiliated (there was a large crowd of spectators) I went home and was determined that this was it. I did not deserve to be treated like this. I was better than this. Just who did he think he was? Better yet, I said to myself, Tara what has happened to you. You have become too soft. How can you let him walk over you like that? Those were the emotions and thoughts flowing through my head.

He came home shortly after I arrived with his mouth full of lies. He begged and pleaded for me not to leave. He said that it was over between them and that was what the fight was about. He denied her ever being pregnant stating she was just trying to "get you mad". As a matter of fact he denied them ever being intimate together. Up until this point I had fell for everything he said, but not this time. I had really had enough. During the previous episodes I had threaten to take our son and move out of state. This time I had really made up my mind to leave.

The officers came to our apartment to get his side of the story. He pleaded with me, not to let the officers know that he was at home. "Tara please they are going to take me to jail" he exclaimed. I went outside and talked with the officers. I remember one of the officers (the one who had asked me to leave earlier) saying "if it was me, I know my wife will have me in the doghouse". Hearing this response, solidified my decision, I no longer cared. He had hurt me for the last time. No longer will I be his doormat. I called my sister Von and asked if my son and I could come and stay with her for a while.

I said to my husband "Johnny we are leaving. I am going to New York to live with my aunt". I did not want him to know that I was really only going to West Palm Beach with my sister. I began packing our clothes. He said that I was not going anywhere. I screamed "I am going you have hurt me long enough". Then he said, "well, you are not taking my picknee (Jamaican term for child) anywhere". The nerve of him, I thought, after causing me all this distress. However, I was thoroughly settled on leaving.

Now my husband had a temper and he was very stubborn. When we were not arguing about his cheating, it would be about me going out to the clubs or playing cards. He would do anything from hiding or destroying my clothes to taking my car keys. The biggest fight would be about my unwillingness to be intimate with him. I had begun to loathe sleeping with him because he had betrayed me and violated our marriage. So when I refused him, he would do anything from hitting me, pushing me, cussing me, or even locking me out the bedroom. So I knew he was serious about not letting me leave. That night (well actually 2 in the morning because she was on her way to work) my sister Barb came to pick me up. He was barricaded in front of the bedroom door with a machete and told me I was not going anywhere. I pleaded desperately for him to let us leave, while hearing my sister's knocks on the door. She eventually left because she had to go to work. The next day he pleaded with me not to leave and convinced me that he wanted the three of us to leave this town and start over. He promised, "Things would be different". So within the month we left town and moved in with my sister.

New Place Same Thing

e lived with my sister for about four months, and then we were able to move into our own apartment. Now he becomes the hero and

wants to help his brother. "Tara if he comes here, he can get a good job". "Just let them come for a while to get on his feet". The brother and the brother girlfriend moved in. The arrangement was working out okay. The couple decided to move back to the girlfriend's hometown.

Johnny now decides to extend the same opportunity to his cousin. Well against better judgment I said okay, mainly because we were just given help from my sister. I figured family really should look out for each other. So the cousin and his girlfriend moved in (now the fun begins).

Shortly after they moved in, I began getting calls from a lady asking for someone named Everton. After a couple of weeks of telling this person they had the wrong number I finally said "the next time you see Everton you need to ask him what his real name is because I have told you there is no Everton living here". She said, "Oh you want to know who I'm talking about,

Everton is short, red, and he drives a black car". I sat quietly as she described my husband. After exchanging a few words with her, I hung up the phone and headed outside to confront "Everton". I walked up to him and asked him who was Everton, "I don't' know" he replied. I then told him he was a liar because the girl just described him and the car he drove. He denied it as he jumped into the car with his cousin and they drove off. About thirty minutes later the girl called back. She said that "Everton" had just left her house cussing her out for calling his house and she was not ever talking to him again. I was mistaken to think that meant he went over there to defend my honor by telling her not to disrespect his wife. In retrospect, I bet he never cussed her at all. Instead they probably laughed while she called to tell me those things, so I would believe that it was over between them.

I believed just about anything that man said. As I now reflect, I wonder how I could have been so naïve. By this time I had channeled my anger toward the relationship between him and his cousin. I associated his philandering ways with his cousin and their quest to prove who could get the most numbers. I secretly wanted them to stop being friends.

The prior events happened during the first three years of our marriage. After the incident with the second lady, I did not have any confrontations with any other women. Now based on his track record, I am sure there were others, but I was never knowingly exposed to them. By the fourth year of our marriage we had moved into a second apartment with his cousin. Things were going pretty good. Even though I had my insecurities, we were getting alone better than ever. I became pregnant with our second son Keinte and we decided it was time to move into our own place. I enrolled in school for Practical Nursing. It looked like we were finally becoming a "normal family".

Life's Curve

On Sunday night March 24th 1996 at about 11pm, I was awakened by a knock at the door. I laid there in the dark, still, thinking they must have the wrong door. The knocking became louder and more intense. I sluggishly aroused from bed and peeped out the window. It was then that I spotted the detective as he stepped off the front porch to look upstairs at the window. I thought oh I better go downstairs, something must be wrong. I wondered if perhaps my family had an accident as they were returning from a trip to Tallahassee visiting my niece. I wobbled (as I was nine months pregnant) down the stairs to see what was the matter. I opened the door after the detectives identified themselves. With the door now ajar, "Is Veronica Johnson your sister" one of the detective asked. Immediately my knees became weak and I began crying. I looked into their faces hoping to hear them say that there was no need to cry, that she was alright. Instead they asked if there was someone else at home with me. By that time Johnny was walking down the stairs. The detectives escorted me into the living room to have a seat. One of the detectives proceeded to tell me that my sister had been found murdered in her apartment, a single gunshot wound to the head. I could not believe what I was hearing. My husband was with the other detective making calls to my family members. I heard him give the detective my sister Vickie's phone number. I tried to tell them not to call her because I knew she would "loose it". But I was frozen; the words could not come out my mouth. I was so perplexed and was thinking, who could have done something like this to her. Then suddenly I thought "Oh, God what about those children". Her kids were ages 9, 8, and 23 months at that time. I still remember the next day when we had to tell them. We decided to let their paternal grandmother break the news. Prior to their grandmother telling them the oldest had seen the news footage and exclaimed, "Ooh Auntie somebody got killed out there where we live"! My heart broke all over again, because I knew we were moments away from telling them that it was their mom.

When it first happened I thought I could not make it. This was the most painful thing I had ever experienced. I had lost both parents by this time, but they had both been sick and suffered for years before passing. But Von was a young, vibrant, 27 year old mother of three. She was my sister; we were to grow old together. She was not supposed to die and especially not alone in her apartment for 2 days as if she had no one who cared about her.

I had my second son 3 days after her body was found. What should have been a joyous time was instead clouded by the tragic event of her death. She had been working the 3-11pm shift and would routinely call me when she got home. About a month before her death, I told her to stop calling waking me up because I had to go to school the following mornings and she wanted to talk all night long. We both laughed but she complied with my request. So over the next few months I went through many different emotions. I was mad, hurt, and confused. I often asked "why". Why did it happen? Why did she move there? Why was she alone? Why did I tell her to stop calling me? I was angry at myself, thinking if I never would have told her to stop calling, maybe this would not have happen. Or perhaps I would have been talking to her and would be able to identify the killer.

For months following her death, these thoughts would plaque my mind. My other two sisters, Barbara and Vickie seemed to have found peace through Jesus. Out of my emotions I decided to try this Jesus. Well I would find out later the key to having a relationship with Jesus. But as for that particular time it did not work out for me. The secret is that after surrendering to Jesus you must get in a Bible teaching church. Study the word of God and commune with Him daily through prayer. I did not know any of that at the time. So the first time I cussed, after my so-called conversion (after only 2 weeks) I thought "oh well, I messed up". I started back willfully practicing sin. See I was not aware of God's word that says in 1 John 1:9 "If we confess our sins, He is faithful and just to forgive us our sins, and to cleanse us from all unrighteousness". I did not know about the Holy Spirit, which would give me the power to stay saved. For the next 5 years I would remain in the "wilderness".

Tragedy,
a Common Place

After my sister's death my family became even closer. We decided that we would spend time with each other more frequently and express our love for one another. We would take her kids on trips and do whatever we could to be supportive to them.

My husband on the other hand was totally opposite. He did not like having my family over all the time. And he did not like me being gone away from home with my family so often. See during that time I was one of those foolish wives, well I certainly was not acting like a Proverbs 31 woman. As women we should help build our husband and our household. In hindsight, I should have asked his permission or his input regarding affairs involving our home. Well that is water under the bridge now. The truth is after losing my sister my siblings and their offspring became a very integral part of my life. I loved my family but my husband did not like to be around "people", his excuse was related to cultural differences. So, the children and I were always hanging out with my family.

About two years after Von was murdered, my sister Barb called me and said "Tara, you need to come over and take a look at Greg" (he was one of our 5 brothers). "Why, what's going on I asked?" He has not been eating and he don't look good" she replied. When we made it over to his house and I saw him my heart felt as if it would fail. He was so thin that he appeared wasted away. We tried to encourage him to get out the house and go for a ride with us, but he refused. He wanted to be left alone. As we left his house I said to my sister "he has AIDS". She angrily asked, "Why do you say that". I retorted, "Because he looks like he does". He eventually was admitted to the hospital. While in the hospital he was given the news that he was HIV positive. We would later find out this was not the first time he had been told that he was positive. In less than a year from that Greg would be dead, approximately 3 years after the murder of our sister.

I remember on New Year's Day (2 months before his death) we had a dinner party at my house. When my family arrived, I looked out of the kitchen window and saw Greg getting out of the car. He was so frail; I felt so much pain for him but was afraid of him at the same time. See, although I was in Practical Nursing School at the time, I still did not know much about HIV. When my family left, I remember purposely putting bleach in my dishwater. Although this was (and still is) a common practice of mine since I was a young girl, I felt the need to make sure I did so that day. Finally I threw away all my blue cups because he had drank from a blue one and I was not sure if the bleach killed "it".

Today I write this as a Registered Nurse working for one of the largest not-for-profit HIV/AIDS providers.

Reflecting back on my brother's condition I really feel bad that he had to shoulder that burden (or secret) alone. I mean as close as our family was, he didn't feel like he could share his condition with any of his siblings. But I am sure that was because of the stigma surrounding HIV/ AIDS. Even today, it still exists, people are whispering, pointing fingers, and some are even laughing. A diagnosis of HIV/AIDS is like a well-kept dirty secret. Only it is not well kept at all, time goes on and infection rates continue to climb. If the stigma is removed more people will seek testing and treatment. More people will share their stories with others. Maybe those infected will feel more safe and comfortable about disclosing their status. This could help reduce the rate of new infections. The Bible says that "God is not willing that any should perish, but that all should come to repentance" (2 Peter 3:9b).

For the African American families, the churches are the pillars of our communities. Most black churches, however, refuse to discuss HIV/AIDS. Perhaps because talking about this disease would lead to conversations about homosexuality, promiscuity, drugs, and sex. Many people have put a taboo sticker on those subjects and do not want to deal with them. Sure HIV/AIDS is mentioned during a sermon or two to describe the punishment for fornication or adultery. And, that's the extinct of church's roll in educating and embracing people with HIV/AIDS. Infected people are sometimes treated like modern day lepers (okay that may be too extreme). But I tell you the truth the way they are being treated (especially by the church) stinks in God's nostril. The basis of Christianity is love and the bible says that love is what draws others (Jeremiah 31:3b). We should walk in love with everyone. You can embrace a person with love without accepting the sin in their life.

It is time we take the blinders off and face this problem head on. Stop pretending it is something that happens to other people. This disease does not discriminate. It crosses every age, race, and religious boundary. It goes into our neighborhoods, our schools, and yes even our churches.

I had a conversation once with a young minister about HIV/AIDS. He said that he did not believe the church should be educating people about HIV/AIDS. He said the only thing the "people" should hear about HIV from the church is that they can be healed. I agree with this in part. I believe that the education regarding HIV/AIDS that comes from the church should include explaining what the disease is, how it is contracted, and about testing (we have not been saved all our lives). Teaching about abstinence and other biblical principles should be the primary focal point. Miracles are real so teaching about God's healing power should definitely be included. These teaching, coming from the church, will give a person so much empowerment and encouragement which will sustain them while they wait on their manifested healing in this life or the one to come.

Changes

As I mentioned before my husband had a temper. One night he became very irate because I refused his advances for intimacy. He began cussing me and proceeded to push then strike me. He stormed down stairs. I was hoping he was leaving. Much to my surprise he returned with a broken broomstick. For the first time, I became deathly frightened. I pleaded with him not to hit me as he swiftly approached me. Without a word he struck me on my leg several times with the stick. I screamed and yelled that I was going to call the police. He left the house and I called the police. I remember thinking that I was fed up and did not care what happened to him at that point. I would no longer allow him to physically assault me.

That night the officers arrived and I told them what happened. I showed them the marks on my leg and the stick he used. The officers told me that because he used a weapon that whether I press charges or not the State would likely "take up" the case. The officers kept the broomstick for evidence. Johnny returned home later that night apologized, but told me once again that it was my fault.

Several months later he received a letter informing him that the State Attorney's office was charging him with domestic battery. He was appointed a public defender that informed him that it would be in his best interest to have me come to court and speak on his behalf. I did attend the court proceedings with him, but did not have to speak. He was placed on probation and had to attend anger management classes. I know it was the Lord's doing because from the time he got in trouble with the law and began those classes he never laid his hands on me again. I remember thinking my God I should have called the police on him seven years ago. While the physical abuse did cease, the verbal continued. That man had a mouth on him. And while I do point out his flaws, I was not blameless because during that time of my life, I had some choice words for him as well.

Unfortunately that had become our norm. Although during this time I had not heard of any more infidelity, but I just did not trust him. I guess I never forgave him and when I would think about what he had done in the past I would become upset. Un-forgiveness breeds misery and bitterness. Overall things were quieting down. I had completed LPN school and started to work. We were making plans to have his teenage son come from Jamaica to live with us.

During this time I had begun to re-examine my life and realized that I really needed a change (Spiritually). I kept promising myself that I was going to start attending church services. But each week I would have some excuse when the appointed time came. I mentioned before that my vice was playing cards (gambling). Each year I would make a New Year's resolution not to gamble anymore. And each year I would probably be the first one to call and get a card game started. However around Christmas time in 1999 I told the ladies I played cards with "this is it", "when the New Year comes in I am not playing cards anymore". They laughed and said, "You say that every year". Much to my own surprise when the New Year began and they called me I said "no" each time until eventually they stopped calling. It is so amazing because when I look back and reflect on it I know it was the Lord that took the habit from me. At the time however, I thought that I was doing it from my own strength.

One week, I finally made up my mind to go the church on the upcoming Sunday. Later in that week I spoke with a friend of mine who invited me to a concert some Jamaican artists were having on that Saturday night. I told her that I could not go because I had promised myself that I was going to church the next day. She told me that I would still be able to go to church. She pleaded with me to come to the concert, promising that I would have a good time. But I knew after going out I would not be in any shape to go to church the next day. Nevertheless, I gave in and told her I would go with her. We made plans where we would meet up on Saturday night. Well that Friday there was sort of a crisis involving my sister Vickie, which caused me to be out of town that weekend. I ended up going to church after all. Me and two of my family members went to the altar for prayer. The ministerial staff working around the altar had my family stand together so the Pastor could pray for us on behalf of my sister. When Pastor Brown laid his hands on me I felt the power of God. I felt myself lift off the ground as if I was floating. I remember saying "nobody ever told me it felt like this".

After that experience, I started going to church regularly. I developed a hunger and I wanted more of God. I accepted Christ as my Savior.

Right Back Where
We Started From

A few months after I became a Christian, I started having problems again with my husband. I watched him slowly become distant. I did

recognize that it was the enemy (devil/satan) using him to distract me from focusing on God. However, I was not equipped with the power (Holy Spirit) at that time. So I began feeling unloved and unwanted. I continued going to church, but I was on an emotional roller coaster. In church I felt good but when I got home those feelings would set in again. Over the next 4 months this man would leave the house on a daily basis. This behavior was far different from the times before. The enemy tried to plant things in my head. I remember thinking one time "you know he is cheating, go out and get you a boyfriend, you can get back "saved" later. For two weeks after that thought I did not go to church. I sat around the house feeling sorry for myself and actually entertained the thought about "getting a boyfriend". I am so grateful that I realized that was not the plan God had for my life. The devil will try to do anything to get you to abort your mission. I resumed going to church and prayed for a change in my marriage.

One weekend while the children were away I decided, tonight will be the night I find out what he has been up to. That evening while he was in the shower I took his phone and ran out to my car. My intentions were to go through the phone in hopes of locating this woman and informing her that she was involved with a married man. Looking back, it was a dumb move, because if someone is no longer in love with you doing something like that does not help your case. In fact it, oftentimes, push them further away. The truth was, however, that I was fed up and desperate. Although I managed to make it to my car and lock myself in, needless to say, he was fast on my trail. He sprung onto the hood of my car and began yelling and pounding for me to open the door. I was so afraid that he was going to break my window; I never even looked at his call logs. Someone called the police and when they arrived they suggested that one of us leave to avoid trouble. You probably guessed it; he used that as his excuse to stay out all night.

I remember calling his phone to no avail that night. At one point I drove around to different apartment complexes looking for his truck. I rode around most of the night and sat up crying for the rest. The next morning was Sunday and as I was heading to church I called his phone again. He answered and told me that it was my fault that he had to stay out all night. He had the nerves to tell me he was out with the woman. He denied being intimate, stating they just talked all night as if that lie made it hurt any less. By the time I got to church my eyes were so red from crying all night. My heart was so heavy as if it would burst. I remember going up for prayer (I wanted the pain to stop) and as I was returning to my seat Sis James walked up to me and embraced me. She did not say a single word but I felt the compassion and concern.

When I returned home that evening from church my husband and his friend Jimmy was at the house. His friend tried to be the mediator and told my husband he was wrong for what he was doing. He said "Johnny, Tara is a good woman; you should not treat her like this". I personally just felt numb. I could not believe that he was willing to throw away 10 years of marriage for someone he had only known for a few months. But based on his behavior I knew his heart had truly turned. Oddly enough he did not leave the house that evening; this was the first time in the past 4 months. I was secretly hoping that maybe he was considering what his friend was saying. Well the next day I would find out that was not the case. The next evening he left the house and did not return that night. The following morning when he came home I lost it. He stepped in the door and I charged him. My kids were yelling "mamma no". Until this day Keinte will declare that we divorced because "you beat my daddy up that morning".

He left for work and to drop his son Kevon off at school. I went to work as well but was so distracted. I left work and came home. I cried, prayed, and cried some more. I remember calling my niece to ask her advice about "putting him out". She said you need to pray and she abruptly said she would have to call me back (because she was at work). So I prayed (but I was not in tune with God's voice) and immediately I called my friend Ginger, who was happy to come help me change the locks. I put his clothes inside his truck while my friend changed the door locks. And would you know it that he came home early this day and caught us changing the locks. He cussed at us and called the police who informed me that I would have to give him a key. So he officially had his license to sleep out every night because "you put me out".

Finally Getting It

By this time my husband had rented an apartment and officially moved out. I was so down and felt so lonely. I once asked him, "Why do you have to treat me so bad, if you no longer wanted me you could have just left, you did not have to get a woman and be so disrespectful". He replied "Tara, what fool quit one job before they find another one". Those words stung my heart and crushed my emotions even more. My mind constantly played the "what if " and "why" game. I cried out for God to strengthen me and take the feelings of malice out of my heart. By this time I had been a Christian for about eight months. I really did not have a strong bible study or prayer life. I would read my bible on Sunday and would not take it out again until the following Sunday. When I prayed it was almost an afterthought. But thank God I belonged to a church with two faithful leaders Pastors Clarence and Cynthia Brown. They preached the word of God and as Pastor Clarence would say, "I preach the raw gospel, I don't sugarcoat it, nothing added and nothing taken away". They preached what we needed, not what we wanted to hear.

God also paired me up with a sister from the church. She was a young woman but "seasoned" in the Lord. Sis Hannah would counsel you via the word of God and like our Pastors she did not compromise God's truth. If you were wrong, she would let you know. I truly thank God for her being such an essential part of my life during what I saw as my "darkest times".

So through their teaching and counseling I realized that I needed the Holy Spirit and that "It" would not dwell in an unclean vessel". I asked God to send the Holy Spirit to dwell in me. We were having a revival at church and that night was going to be "Holy Ghost" night. I stayed home from work that day and fasted and prayed. I confessed my unresolved feelings toward my husband and his mistreatment of me. I asked God to place love and forgiveness in my heart. That night at church I received the baptism of the Holy Spirit. I was now equipped with the power for survival, not only to survive but to LIVE. My life was not the same after that night. I noticed that some things that bothered me before did not bother me any longer. I was now able to sleep at night. No longer would I lay awake wondering why. God was strengthening me through the Holy Spirit, which had become my comforter, my friend, my peace, and my lover.

About six months after he had moved out, I returned home from church and much to my surprise the man had moved back in. He never asked me if he could come home, he just showed up with his belongings. I had mixed emotions because although I still wanted my husband, I did not want to be sharing him. The woman he was dating was from his native homeland. I eventually surmised that she had returned there and that was why he came back home. I remember saying, oh I guess he figured; "it's cheaper to keep me". Now I will give him credit for one thing and that was being a provider for the family. He had always worked and took care of his responsibilities. That is why during the times he would fight me I would never call the police. I did not want him to get arrested and perhaps lose his job.

He was back in the house but he was still so distant. Although he was home all the time now, "his body was there but his mind was somewhere else". He spent most of his time on the phone or hanging outside our apartment with his son or his friend. After two months I moved into another apartment. He told me that he and his friend would keep the old apartment. I was glad because the more I studied the Bible I realized that this was not the way God ordained a marriage to be and "I DESERVED MORE".

Two weeks later he would show up and ask to move in. I originally said no. He pleaded saying that his friend decided not to move into the apartment with him and he promised he would only be there "for a little while". A part of me wanted things to work out. I allowed him to move in and things were pretty much the same.

Two months later he was still in my apartment. He and his cousin were planning a trip to Jamaica for Christmas. He would be gone for one week. I felt myself getting so sad because I knew he was only going to spend time with the woman. My breaking point was when he was gone that man called the house once on Christmas Eve night and spoke briefly with the kids and me. I believe I cried the whole time he was gone. I keep thinking suppose something happen to the kids or me. And my God his own son was here as well; sure he was eighteen years old by then, but never the less that was his child. The next time

I would talk to him would be the early morning of New Year's Day. After returning from church I was greeted with "Happy New Year Tara" he said while lying on the couch. I was so angry with both him and myself. I was mad at how disrespectful he had become and at myself for allowing him to control me emotionally.

I remember feeling so lonely and longing to be loved by my husband. I really did not think I could feel so empty with a spouse in the house with me. I was so consumed with my husband's love (or lack thereof) that I would go to bed thinking about him and wake up thinking about him. I would cry out to God asking Him to intervene, fix it, quicken it, Lord please save my marriage. After a while I found myself unable to pray for my marriage any longer. I began praying for peace. Then God revealed to me the scripture Matthew 6:33 "but seek ye first the kingdom of God and His righteousness and all these things will be added unto you".

See I had been so caught up with wanting man to love me and was missing out on the true love of Jesus Christ. On two occasions, while driving down the road crying and asking "Lord why this man doesn't love me, why do he treat me this way"? I looked up and saw a plane writing "Jesus Loves You" in the sky. After the second time I remember laughing out loud saying Thank You Jesus. It became clear at that point, I finally put it together. I realized that God was telling me to seek Him and put my trust in Him for He cared for me. I made a conscious decision to "get on with my life". I became more involved with church, going to Sunday school, Bible study, and any other activities that would keep me around positive, spirit filled people. I started studying my bible, fasting, and praying even more.

Empowered

O nce my focus truly turned toward God and His love for me I found myself not so easily moved by things that my husband did. I transferred

my passion away from my toxic relationship with my husband, toward a closer one with the Lord.

One morning Johnny and I were having some words before I left for work. I was tired of him being at home, but not really "being there". I took the yellow pages and open it up to divorce lawyers and told him "knock yourself out". He called me later at work to tell me he found a paralegal. Truthfully, my first reaction was that of relief. So he filed for divorce and a couple months later he moved into his own apartment. He tried to manipulate me by stalling the divorce proceeding and when he was upset he would turn in another paper and we would become a step closer to the final proceeding. Even after all he had taken me through; I really was hoping he would change his mind. But eventually we got the papers to come to court for the finalization. The day the sheriff officer brought the papers I sat to my dining room table and I cried. Later that day I received a call from someone from the blood bank. "Mrs. Harris, it has been three months since you donated blood and we was hoping you would come and donate some more". I finished my conversation with the lady and as I sat there I began to rejoice. I said Lord I thank you because they could have been calling me to tell me that they had to reject my donation. That's when it hit me that this man had probably been unfaithful throughout the twelve years we were married. And while earlier I had been crying, because the divorce would soon be finalized, I realized that I should be rejoicing that God "covered me".

Prior to the finalization of the divorce we had to go to mediation. We received a packet to complete regarding custody of the kids and the division of our assets. That was easy because we really did not have any assets. We would both keep our own vehicles. We would be responsible for any liabilities that were in our individual name. The contents of each bank account would belong solely to whose name was on it. We no longer had a joint bank account because of my history of gambling and frivolous spending. On the other hand, he had always been a saver. Over the past couple years prior to the divorce he had saved up over twenty thousand dollars. I told him I did not want any of his money, but I made sure he knew I was "entitled" to half. When we arrived at mediation he presented some bogus check stubs, reflecting that he was being paid much less than he actually was. I was mad and everything in me wanted to say "he is lying". I also wanted to change and request half of the money from his account. The Holy Spirit kept telling me to be still. I was annoyed but I keep quiet. A peace began to come over me as I realized that the one thing that remained consistent throughout the entire transition was him being there for the boys. I never had to "run him down" or beg him to provide support for them. We got through mediation without incident.

Several weeks later, we went to court for the finalization of the divorce. When we arrived in the courtroom the judge began by asking my husband some questions. He was so nervous that he could not coherently answer. The judge said, "Okay let's try this again". He then turned to me and asked about our children, where we married, and finally how long had we been married. He also pointed out that the petition for divorce was filed with us both using the same address. He asked if we were sure that the marriage was irretrievably broken. I stammered um, no, well um yes (inside I was screaming "help, send us to counseling, save my marriage"). He asked me if I would be reverting back to my maiden name and with that it was officially over. As we left the courthouse he said, "See how you divorced me". I said boy you are crazy and we both laughed, but inside I was crying. After leaving the court I met Sis Hannah for lunch. I said, "Well it's official, I'm back on the market". She replied, "I didn't realize this was the final hearing". We sat there talking for about two hours and although I had a smile on my face I felt rejected and useless.

Liberation

The divorce was final and I was now a "statistic", another divorced, mother of two. While I should have been rejoicing for my freedom, I found myself feeling ashamed. I really felt "worthless" because how could someone divorce a "woman of God". I believe one of the primary reasons that I did not want to get divorced was because we had been married for over ten years before I became a Christian. I had learned so much since becoming "saved". I realized that although I was never unfaithful to him, I still had not been the virtuous woman. As I mentioned before I had a problem with gambling and saving money, which caused a lot of problems in our marriage. So I wanted to show him the "new and improved, spirit-filled" me. I felt that I was letting the Lord down because this man had divorced me.

One day when I was really feeling down about the divorce, I began communing with the Lord. Suddenly I felt the presence of the Lord come into my room. During prayer I was lead to the Bible scripture that says "But if the unbelieving depart, let him depart. A brother or a sister is not under bondage in such cases: but God hath called us to peace" (1 Corinthian 7:15). Oh this blessed my soul so much. I finally realized that I did not need to feel guilty or ashamed. The man no longer wanted me and he had moved on. I said "oh well, it's his loss". I continued to spend time with the one person that loved me and had always been there for me. My Lord and I were inseparable.

Stand Still

After being divorced for about a year and a half, my ex called me. He said "Tara, I just wanted you to know how much I see the glow of God on you". He apologized and told me how he had made a big mistake. He continued by saying, "If God does not let us marry back to each other then I hope you never get married again". I was both humored and shocked by his statement. This was the first time since I had known him that he expressed what appeared to be genuine remorse. At this point I had forgiven him and was getting on with my life. But I did get a sense of gratification that he had realized that the grass was not so green on the other side after all. He said that he wanted to buy a house for the boys and myself. He went on to explain that he had always promised to buy me one while we were married. He was now in the position and it was the least he could do. He said he would make the mortgage payments in lieu of child support. I told him that I accepted his apology, but he was no longer obligated to purchase a house for me. He insisted. After talking it over with a couple Christian friends, it occurred to me that it was because of my humbleness during our divorce why God would even allow this man to make such an offer.

A year earlier while I was at the COGIC Holy Convocation attending the midnight musical, this gentleman asked if he could pray with me. He started ministering to me by saying "God said don't let your heart be troubled, He took y'all apart so that when y'all come back together, things will be much better". He also told me that he see me moving into a new house. Now I took this to mean that God had caused my ex and I to depart and he would unite us again and things would be better. Despite how he had treated me, I never wanted the divorce, but I did want things to change. Oddly enough things had changed between us. He treated me with more respect than he ever had and we had become friends. Now because of my relationship with the Lord at that time, I would not allow myself to drift. I drew the line, because we were divorced and he had someone else. Actually he had the woman that he had left me for. But God had purged all the hurt, shame, and anger out of me and I felt good. God had grown me in the midst of what had been my affliction. So when my ex came to me about buying the house I initially said no, then I thought about what the gentleman had ministered to me and thought, "God, can this really be it". I now realize that we can get caught up on the promise of God and try to make "it" happen ourselves. But when God promise you something, you just stay in position, because it will come to pass. But when you move ahead of God and try to put it together yourself, it falls apart every time. This was a hindsight revelation and I will share that experience with you in my next book. But for now I will resume this story.

I agreed with him purchasing the house. The deal on the initial house he attempted to purchase fell through at the last minute. Several days later, he called me and asked for my bank account number. I inquired as to why he needed it. He told me he was closing out his bank account and putting the money into my account for my house. "Say what" I thought, the same money the enemy tried to get me to fight about during mediation. God will work all things out for your good.

Isaiah 61:3 To appoint unto them that mourn in Zion, to give unto them Beauty for Ashes, the oil of joy for mourning, the garment of praise for the spirit of heaviness; that they might be called trees of righteousness, the planting of the LORD, that he might be glorified.

At times when you feel alone, just know that Jesus is near. He's always there and will never leave you. Just trust Him to see you through. No matter what situation you are facing, let Him take the lead, to guide you. He provides all the love we need and has given us all things that pertain to life and Godliness (2 Peter 1:3). His love is unconditional and with it you are able to have success in all areas of your life. After you have been tried by the fire, you shall come forth as pure gold (Job 23:10). God will truly give you "Beauty for Ashes", oh what an exchange!

RESOURCES

Domestic Violence Resources:

National Domestic Violence Hotline 1-800-799-SAFE
(7233)
http://www.ndvh.org

U.S. Department of Justice Office on Violence Against
Women 1-202-307-6026
http://www.ojp.usdoj.gov/vawo

National Network to End Domestic Violence
1-202-543-5566
www.nnedv.org

AIDS/HIV Resources:
AIDS Healthcare Foundation 1-323-860-5200
www.aidshealth.org

www.aids.gov